OLD FISHING
TACKLE
And Collectibles

OLD FISHING TACKLE
and Collectibles

Dan Homel

Forrest - Park Publishers
Bellingham, Washington

ISBN: 1 - 879522 - 02 - 0

CREDITS

Electronic pre-press and cover mechanicals
prepared by Marcus Yearout.
Photographs: Dan Homel
Darkroom work: Quicksilver Photo Lab.
Printer: Thomson-Shore

Special Thanks to Harold Jellison for his valuable assistance and friendship. Also my sincere appreciation to members of the N.F.L.C.C., who have been so encouraging in the past. To my family and friends who have provided great moral support for my writing work over the years, thanks again.

To
Jan, Joe, Will, and Atessa

Preface

Twenty years ago, only a handful of people collected old fishing tackle, and the opportunities to build a collection of rods, reels or lures seemed endless. Every auction, swap meet or garage sale yielded something good. Now that the hobby has grown, naturally it is a bit more difficult to locate collectible tackle at every turn. But do not despair, the hobby is still young, the ranks of tackle collectors have not yet reached staggering numbers, and much old tackle remains!

It is true that fishermen and non-angler alike are aware of the popularity of tackle from the past, and prices have gone up since I began collecting in the early 1970's. However, most old fishing tackle is still reasonably priced (compared to other sporting collectibles) because seasoned collectors concentrate on the "rarest and oldest". This leaves the bulk of fishing collectible items within the budget of the average enthusiast.

Many antique malls and shops now have displays of old tackle, and dealers eagerly look for fishing stuff because they know it is salable. As a result, old rods, reels and lures that would have otherwise remained in a garage or attic, are made available to collectors.

It has been three years since I wrote Collector's Guide to Old Fishing Reels. Based on the positive response I continue to receive from that project (going into it's second printing), and requests from both collectors and book distributors, we offer you this book on all types of tackle - from rods and reels to hooks and creels! We hope the information is helpful.

Dan Homel
Bellingham, Washington

Contents

Fishing Accessories

Angling Ephemera

FISHING RODS

Antique Wood Rods

In the earliest times, fishing rods were fashioned from tree limbs or branches and used for "dapping" - a method pre-dating the reel and winch. A line of horse tail or woven thread was simply attached to the rod tip and dangled along with a handmade, baited hook or lure.

With the passing of centuries, rod making became more refined with rounding, smoothing or beveling of the wood. Further improvements were the addition of reel seats, sectioning of the rod, and the advent of true ferrules.

During the mid-1800's American hickory and ash were common rod materials, along with imported greenheart wood. Greenheart was the preferred material of English rod builders and remained so for many years, notwithstanding the development of the split bamboo rod.

American made, wood rods of the Civil War era are found by collectors on occasion, though they are becoming more scarce. These can be recognized because they resemble a billiard "cue stick" and have been so nicknamed. The handle is composed of wound rattan or turned wood, and varnished. The fittings include nickel silver "trumpet" style guides and an agate filled tip top.

Greenheart and ash fly rods of the 1870's will also include rattan or wood handles and come equipped with *Pritchard patent* flip ring guides. Ferrules are sometimes brass and "spiked" in style.

Wood endured as a blank material for big game rods into the

1930's , as evidenced by the very collectible Edward Vom Hofe products.

Split Bamboo Fly Rods

The search for a fly rod material with the characteristics of strength and resiliency (loading power) led to the craft of splitting, sectioning, and gluing bamboo (cane). Some early bamboo rods from Europe consisted of a greenheart wood butt section and bamboo tip section. The cane was of the calcutta variety and usually constructed with two to four beveled strips glued together. These early calcutta rods will have a mottled appearance which is not as uniform in color as the Chinese tonkin cane of later rods. Historic rods of this nature were produced or distributed by Forrest of Kelso, Hardy, Farlow of London, and Robertson of Glasgow.

An interesting ancestor of the modern day pack rod is the valise or "poacher's" rod of four sections or more. Usually enclosed in a small leather case, or concealed in a walking stick, a poacher's rod of greenheart and calcutta makes a nice addition to any antique rod collection.

Perfection and significant advancement in the art of constructing fly rods, made entirely of bamboo, is universally credited to the American craftsman. Although there has been considerable debate on the subject, it is generally thought that Samuel Phillipe, from Pennsylvania, was the first American to produce a split bamboo rod. Phillipe and other Americans, including Charles Murphy and Hiram Leonard, made rods of six strips by the 1870's. However , it was Leonard who established the first true rod factory, in New York, prior to the start of the 20th century. This was the golden age of rod building and each component was created by hand, from the smooth guides to the beautiful knurled reel seat rings.

During the period from World War One to the 1930's, skilled craftsmen such as Ed Payne, F. E. Thomas, and the Edwards family continued the great east coast tradition and made additional contributions to the rod builder's art.

Later, "western" makers such as E.C. Powell and Lew Stoner (Winston) of California, Paul Young of Michigan, and Bill Phillipson of Colorado produced fine rods with their own special characteristics and designs (particularly the fast tip action so popular with anglers of this region).

About the time of World War Two, The Orvis Company of Vermont (with the help of head rod builder Wes Jordan) developed a bakelite impregnation process that sealed the cane fibers from harmful moisture. These durable, popular rods are still made today.

Bill Phillipson also turned out impregnated cane in the 1950's and these, along with his earlier varnished rods, are considered to be a good buy on the second hand rod market.

Mass production of bamboo rods became possible with the creation of automation and the beveling machine, which planed the individual cane strips to the required sixty degree angles. Assembly line rods marketed by South Bend, H & I, Montague, and Shakespeare generally are found to be of lower quality. However, the Wright & McGill *Granger* series and Heddon trout rods (for example model #17 *Black Beauty*) can be exceptionally good due to the fine tapers and installation of more costly nickel-silver ferrules.

Impeccable rods made in low numbers were sold in the 1950's and 60's by the heralded makers Gillum, Dickerson, and Garrison. These rods are now in the highest price range of angling collectibles. Will the values of select fly rods someday rival those of collectible shotguns?

Buying Bamboo Fly Rods

Buying used split bamboo fly rods can be a risky business for the uninformed to engage in. One small imperfection can drastically effect the collectible value of a rod. Things to look out for are:

(1) Defects in the fittings such as cracked ferrules (often at the seam), loose ferrules, rusted guides, bent or broken reel seat, and sometimes less obvious to spot - incorrectly replaced or non-original parts.

(2) Integrity of the bamboo- for example short or broken sections (especially tips), delamination at the glue lines, hook "digs", and bad sets or "bows".

(3) Cosmetic appearance - problems can include refinish or over-varnish (original finish is best), frayed guide wrappings, cracked or "crazed" varnish, soft varnish, and damaged cork.

Even a non-original case or missing rod sack can diminish value and long term investment potential.

A word about tips. Most better quality American fly rods came with two tips (exceptions include early Winston and some Orvis models). Quite a few British rods came equipped with only one tip. If the canvas rod bag appears to be original, count the number of slots to determine if a tip is missing. (i.e. a three piece, two tip rod bag would have four slots).

If you acquire a good rod that needs to be repaired or refinished, don't do it yourself and don't send it to the "local handyman"! If you like this sort of project, find a cheap rod to work on for fun. I have seen many valuable rods ruined by scraping, sanding, chopping, over varnishing, over heating in an attempt to remove sets and ... not to mention horrible, thick epoxy coated re-wraps. A safe bet is to contact a contemporary cane rod builder who also does refinishing.

Remember, old bamboo rods are everywhere to be found - but high quality, valuable bamboo rods are hard to find! Seventy-five percent of the rods that I come across have little collectible value. On the other hand, what is it worth to you? A worn out, broken but unaltered rod from the 1920 era Montague or Horrocks-Ibbotson line, fitted in it's original case and labeled bag, often has great charm. Or consider the post World War Two Japanese made rods; the kind that come in a neat jointed wood box with hooks, flies, and bright graphics label. Rods of this nature can be worth more to the casual collector than the hard core bamboo aficionado. So if you decide to buy one at a price higher than a book such as this subjectively recommends - enjoy it!

Casting, Spinning, and Big Game Rods

Leonard, Orvis, Payne, and Thomas all made bamboo casting or canoe rods of exceptional quality. Bamboo bait casting rods produced by these famous makers were generally available on a custom basis or in low numbers, consequently they are becoming more scarce. Prices are still reasonable, however, compared to fly rods of this caliber! Heddon manufactured great bamboo bait casting rods that are popular collectibles today. Most had a cork fore-grip handle, but some were adorned with a beautiful hardwood handle. Heddons are usually found with an attractive "leaping bass" decal on the shaft and come enclosed in a canvas case with a reinforced tip compartment.

Probably the best bamboo spinning rods were the ultra-light Orvis' and their *Rocky Mountain* combination spin-fly series. Most bamboo spinning rods (Uslan, South Bend, and the heavier Orvis') are simply too "clubby" or poorly set up to balance with an appropriate spinning reel. As a result, except for the lightest American made models and some of the older British examples, bamboo spinning rods are not enthusiastically pursued by most collectors.

If you like to collect saltwater and big game rods, keep an eye out for the Edward Vom Hofe brand, Tycoon Tackle, or the better Montagues in near mint or mint condition. Well worn, broken bamboo saltwater rods are common so condition is everything in this category. Some fine cane steelhead and salmon (mooching) rods were made by Phillipson and Heddon around 1950. Collectors never seem to part with more than $75 to acquire one, so I would count them as a bargain.

Steel and Fiberglass Rods

Solid and tubular steel fishing rods of all types were marketed during the 1920's to 1950's. Of course, these are unpleasant pieces of equipment to actually use, however they make curious, inexpensive collectibles. Bristol, Richardson, Gephart, True Temper, and Shakespeare steel rods were fairly well distributed in North America.

Heddon and Winchester even produced steel rods with a simulated "bamboo" painted finish that is surprisingly realistic in appearance!

Looks are one thing, but what about rod action and lightness? Well, a Heddon ad in the June, 1938 issue of <u>Field and Stream</u> proclaimed: "Shut your eyes and you cannot tell the ... new Pal Steel Rod from a fine bamboo". Most collectors today will disagree with this statement, but some old timers still swear by their trusty steel rods. Nevertheless, the average steel rod is not worth a ten dollar bill. Higher prices are justified for steel rods with built -in reels.

After World War Two, as bamboo production costs escalated, tackle manufacturers began experimenting with fiberglass as a rod material. The first "glass" rods were solid or very thick walled with an action reminiscent of steel. For this reason, early fiberglass rods are virtually worthless as collectibles today. In fact, the widely used production rods of the 1960's from Garcia, Fenwick, and Lamiglas hold only "fishing value".

Discontent with the stiffness and high cost of modern graphite fly rods, some angler-collectors are now searching for used custom quality fiberglass rods. Those made by Russ Peak of Pasadena, California can bring several hundred dollars at auction in mint condition. Also, Winston fiberglass fly rods of the 1970's are considered to be excellent fishing tools, along with the Orvis *Golden Eagle* series.

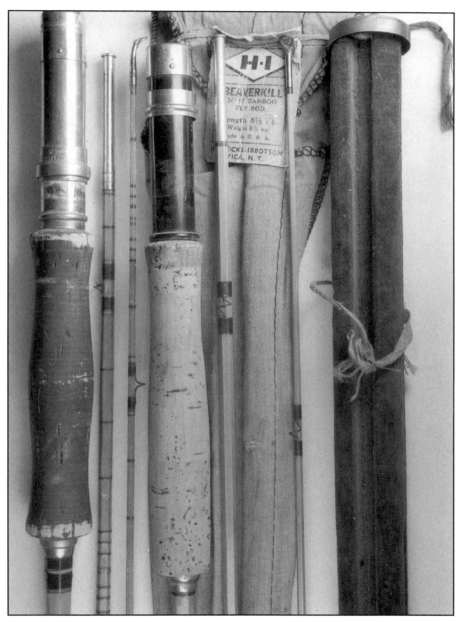

Horrocks-Ibbotson bamboo fly rods. Beaverkill model c.1940-1950 and older trout rod with intermediate wraps c.1920.

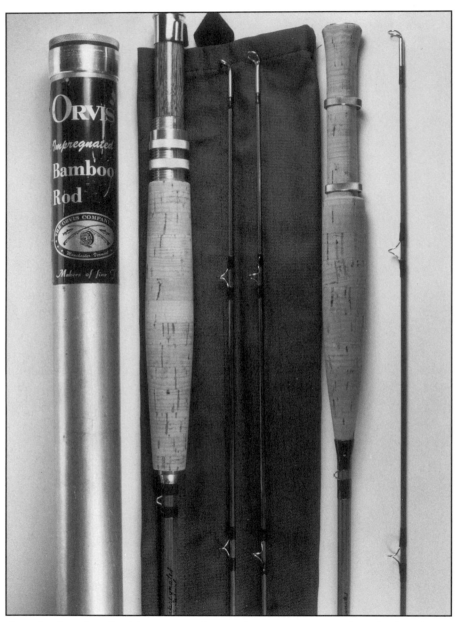

Orvis bamboo fly rods of the 1960s and 70s. 8^1/$_2$' "Limestone Special" and 6^1/$_2$' "Flea." Both rods are bakelite impregnated.

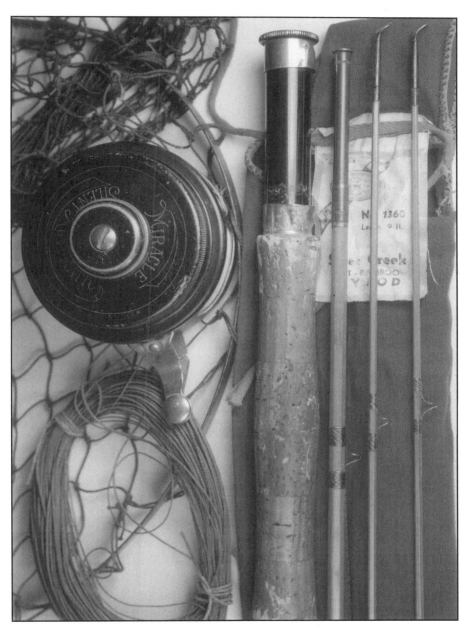

South Bend bamboo fly rod - Silver Creek #1360 with South Bend automatic fly reel and old silk line.

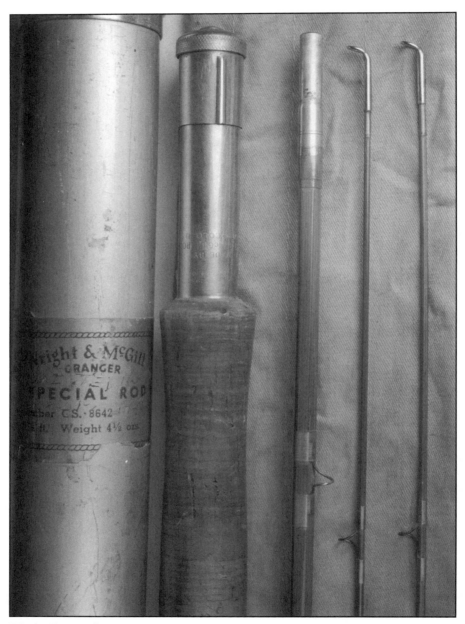

Wright & McGill Granger "Special" bamboo fly rod in original labeled tube. Patented (1938) screw-down reel seat.

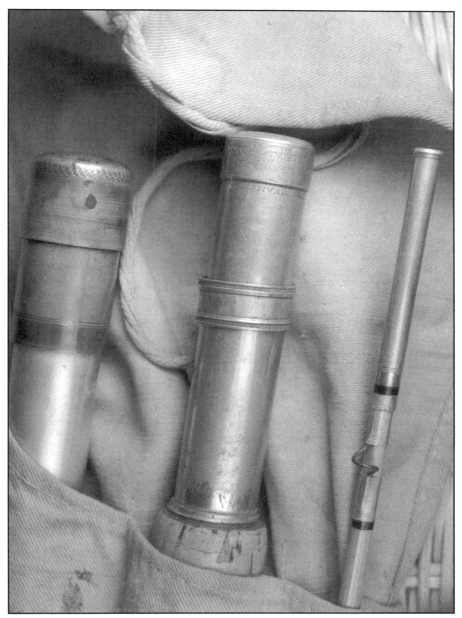

H.L. Leonard "Tournament" bamboo trout rod with aluminum tip tube and canvas bag, (c.1915). Early patented ferrules.

Payne's Handmade Rods

PAYNE'S 3 PIECE FLY RODS

Built of dark bamboo with extra tip. Cork handle, metal or wood reel seat, first guide agate. Balance of guides hardened steel, snake pattern. Perfection or agate tip tops. Hand drawn oxidized German Silver Waterproofed ferrules. Packed in cloth bag and aluminum case.

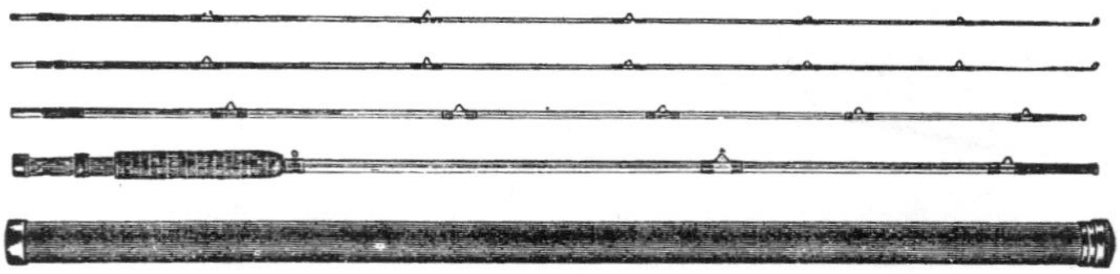

No. 202	8 feet—3¾ to 4¼ ounces		Each	$50.00
No. 204	8½ feet—4¼ to 4¾ ounces		Each	50.00
No. 208	9 feet—4¾ to 5¼ ounces		Each	50.00
No. 210	9½ feet—5¼ to 5¾ ounces		Each	50.00
Extra Butt Joints			Each	19.00
Extra Middle Joints			Each	13.00
Extra Tip Joints			Each	9.25

PAYNE'S 2 PIECE FLY RODS

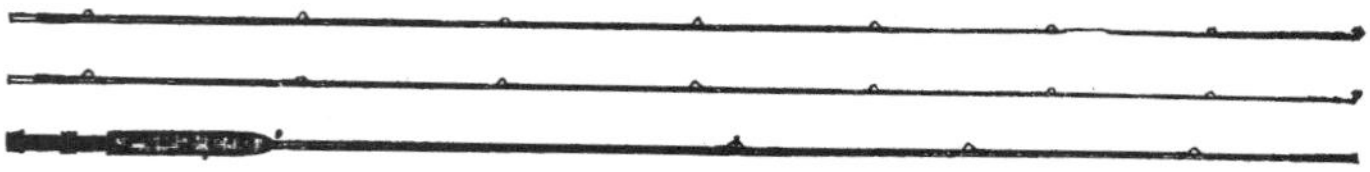

With Extra Tip Joint Made up as Above

No. 100	7½ feet—2½ to 2¾ ounces		Each	$50.00
No. 102	8 feet—3⅞ to 4¼ ounces		Each	50.00
No. 104	8½ feet—4¼ to 4¾ ounces		Each	50.00
Extra Butt Joints			Each	23.50
Extra Tip Joints			Each	13.75

TWO PIECE BAIT CASTING ROD

With short butt joint 28 in., long tip joints 40 in. dark finished split bamboo. German silver reel seat, all agate guides and agate tiptop. Artistic silk winding on guides only. Shaped cork double grip.

No. 302 5½ ft., light, medium and heavy, 4½ to 5½ ounces............Each $38.00

VALUE GUIDE
OLD FISHING RODS

Prices are for bamboo or wood rods in very good to excellent original condition in the original bag and/or case. Mint condition in the original packaging may warrant a higher price. Worn condition with no case, broken condition, or refinished rods should be valued at only 30 - 50% of listed price.

Abbey & Imbrie
Antique calcutta cane fly rod 10' - 2 tips . . . .$200 - 325
(Heddon made) c.1930 fly rod 9' - 2 tips . . . . .90 - 185
Centennial fly rod 9 1/2' (c.1917) - 2 tips . . . . .135 - 225

Abercromby & Fitch
Yellowstone fly rod 8 1/2 - 9' (2 tips) . . . . .125 - 195
Favorite (Edwards built c.1950) 7 1/2' - 2 tips . . . . .195 - 275
Jim Payne fly rods (A & F brand) . . . . .600 and up

Bristol (Edwards)
Model F - 18 (3 piece) fly rod 8 1/2' - 2 tips . . . . .165 - 240

Constable - England
Empress fly rod 8' - 2 tips . . . . .150 - 265
Wallop Brook (staggered ferrule) 7 1/2' - 1 tip . . . . .110 - 190

Thomas Chubb Co.
Ash boat rod c.1880 w/ trumpet guides 8' . . . . .65 - 125
Lancewood fly rod c.1890 10' . . . . .60 - 100
calcutta bamboo fly rod c.1900 . . . . .100 - 190

F. Devine Rod Co.
Antique wood rods 10 1/2' - 2 tips . . . .$75 - 125
Average Devine bamboo fly rod 9' - 2 tips . . . . .150 - 295

Dickerson
Any Dickerson fly rod - especially 7 - 8' . . . . .1000 and up

Dunton
Montague hardware fly rod 7 - 8 1/2' 2 tips . . . . .125 - 200

Edwards
E.W. Edwards (Mt. Carmel) fly rod 7 - 7 1/2' . . . . .500 and up
E.W. Edwards fly rod 8 1/2 - 9' .275 - 425
Bill Edwards Quadrate fly rods 8' . . . . .395 - 495
Edwards spinning rods 6 - 7' 2 tips . . . . .90 - 175

Farlow- England
Antique salmon fly rod (calcutta) c.1900 . . . . .150 - 250
Lee Wulff model 6' fly rod - 2 tips . . . . .295 - 395

Goodwin Granger
Average fly rod 8 1/2 - 9' 2 tips (i.e "champion") . . . . . . .195 - 295

Granger (Wright & McGill)
Special fly rod 9' - 2 tips . . . . .225 - 300
Victory fly rod 8 - 8 1/2' 2 tips .195 - 295
Victory fly rod 7 - 7 1/2' 2 tips .395 - 500
Favorite fly rod 8' - 2 tips . . . . .295 - 375
Favorite fly rod 9' - 2 tips . . . . .175 - 275

Gillum
Any Pinky Gillum fly rod . . . . .2000 and up

Garrison
Any E. Garrison fly rod . . . . .2500 and up

Hardy - England
Wanless spinning rods c.1935 . . . .$95 - 175
Deluxe Palakona fly rod 8' - 2 tips . . . . .185 - 325
Salmon Deluxe fly rod 9' - 2 tips .135 - 250
Phantom Fly rod 9' - 1 tip . . . . .150 - 265
Marvel fly rod 7 1/2' - 2 tips . . . . .300 - 500
J.J. Hardy Triumph fly rod 9' - 2 tips . . . . .135 - 250

Heddon
Bamboo casting rods (i.e model #600) . . . . .60 - 110
#10 fly rod 9' - 2 tips . . . . .65 - 140
#14 fly rod 8 1/2' - 2 tips . . . . .75 - 150
#17 fly rod 8 1/2 - 9' 2 tips . . . . .125 - 225
#17 fly rod 7 1/2 - 8' 2 tips . . . . .240 - 395
#50 fly rod 8 1/2' - 2 tips . . . . .165 - 275
#125 expert 8 1/2 - 9' 2 tips . . . . .175 - 310

Horrocks - Ibbotson Co.
"Expert" model cane casting rod 5 1/2' . . . . .20 - 55
"The Skipper" bamboo boat rod 6' .18 - 30
Tonka Queen or Prince fly rod 7 - 7 1/2' . . . . .90 - 165
Cascade fly rod 8 1/2' - 2 tip . . . . .45 - 85
Governor fly rod 9' - 2 tips . . . . .40 - 75

Howells
7 1/2' #5 fly rod - 2 tips . . . . .550 - 700
8 1/2' # 6 fly rod - 2 tips . . . . .500 - 675

Leonard
Model 37 Catskill series . . . . .1000 and up
Model 38L fly rod 7' - 2 tips . . . . .850 and up
Model 49 fly rod 7 1/2' - 2 tips . . . . .800 and up
Model 50 DF fly rod 8' - 3pc. 2 tips . . . . .750 and up
Tournament 8 1/2' trout fly rod - 2 tips . . . . .350 - 700
Tournament 9' Salmon fly rod - 2 tips . . . . .200 - 425

Mills Standard trout fly rod 8' - 2 tips . . . .$350 - 595
Duracane fly rod 7 1/2' - 2 tips .365 - 550
Antique Salmon fly rod c.1900 (10') . . . . .275 - 375

Montague
Manitou casting rod 5' c.1930 . . . . .25 - 50
Manitou fly rod 9 1/2' - 2 tips . . . . .75 - 135
Splitswitch casting rod 5' - 2 tips .20 - 40
Flash fly rod 8' - 2 tips . . . . .40 - 85
Rapidan fly rod - 2 tips . . . . .45 - 90
Redwing fly rod 9' - 2 tips . . . . .60 - 125
(L.L.Bean label) fly rod 9 1/2' - 2 tips . . . . .65 - 135

Orvis
Spinning rods 6 1/2 - 7 1/2' with 1 tip . . . . .110 - 245
Rocky Mt. fly - spin combo . . . . .225 - 325
Battenkill fly rods 7 - 8 1/2' with 2 tips . . . . .295 - 475
Deluxe fly rod 6 1/2' - 2 tips . . . . .325 - 495
Wes Jordan models with leather case . . . . .450 - 675
"Light Salmon" fly rod 9' - 2 tips . . . . .195 - 295
Shooting Star salmon rods 9' - 2 tips . . . . .210 - 350
Madison / MCL fly rods all with 1 tip only . . . . .185 - 300
Model 99 fly rods - 1 tip . . . . .175 - 295
Bait casting rods - 1 tip . . . . .150 - 250
Antique C. F. Orvis fly rods c.1900 - 1 tip . . . . .180 - 375

Partridge - England
Trout fly rods 7 - 8' with 2 tips .175 - 285
Trout fly rods 7 - 8' with 1 tip . . . . .140 - 210

Payne (Ed or Jim)
Bait casting rods . . . . .265 - 475
Salmon Fly rods . . . . .400 and up
Trout fly rods . . . . .1000 and up

Pezon et Michel - France
Fly rods (staggered ferrules) - 2 tips . . . .$225 - 395

Powell
E.C. Powell 7 1/2 - 8 1/2' trout rods - 2 tips . . . . .450 - 650
E.C. Powell 9 1/2' Steelhead rods - 2 tips . . . . .425 - 625
Walton Powell 9' Steelhead rods - 2 tips . . . . .400 - 500

Phillipson Rod Co.
Pacemaker 8 - 8 1/2' fly rod - 2 tips . . . . .175 - 325
Peerless 7 1/2 - 8 ' fly rod - 2 tips . . . . .195 - 375
Power pakt 7 1/2 - 8 1/2' fly rod - 2 tips . . . . .195 - 375
Paragon fly rod 8 1/2' - 2 tips .175 - 325

Shakespeare
Spring Brook fly rod 8 1/2' c.1950 - 2 tips . . . . .40 - 85
Favorite fly rod 9' c. 1930 - 2 tips . . . . .50 - 95

South Bend
#62 L bamboo casting rod 4 1/2 - 5 1/2' . . . . .15 - 35
#77 bamboo fly rod 9' - 2 tips .65 - 125
#25 Sport Oreno fly rod 7 1/2' - 2 tips . . . . .125 - 190
#24 fly rod 9' c.1935 - 2 tips .75 - 135
#57 fly rod 8 1/2' - 2 tips . . . . .75 - 135
#346 fly rod 8 1/2' - 2 tips .65 - 125
Cross Double Built (early) 9' - 2 tips . . . . .110 - 175

F.E. Thomas
Bangor 8' fly rod - 2 tips . . . . .295 - 450
Browntone 7 1/2' fly rod - 2 tips . . . . .750 and up
Browntone 8 1/2' fly rod - 2 tips . . . . .495 -695
Special 8 1/2' fly rod - 2 tips . . . . .350 - 495
Dirigo 9' fly rod . . . . .275 - 395
Large 10' Salmon fly rods - 2 tips . . . . .195 - 350

Thomas & Thomas
Trout fly rods c. 1970 - present - 2 tips . . . .$425 - 595

Vom Hofe
Heddon produced fly rod 9' - 2 tips . . . . .185 - 295
Edwards produced fly rod 8' - 2 tips . . . . .295 - 395
Big Game - bamboo boat rods . . . . .125 - 250
Antique wood boat rod . . . . .100 - 195

Winston
Lew Stoner made in San Francisco 9' - 1 tip . . . . .295 - 425
R.L. Winston (Montana) 9' - 2 tips . . . . .365 - 495
R.L Winston trout fly rods & 1/2 - 8'(2 tips) . . . . .395 - 595

Winchester
Edwards built 9' trout rod - 2 tips . . . . .175 - 295
Armax brand 9' fly rod - 2 tips . . . . .125 - 225
Barney & Berry (early) . . . . .150 - 250

Wood rods - Civil War Era
Cue Stick hickory rod with flip ring guides . . . . .65 - 175

Paul Young
Parabolic # 15 fly rod 8' - 2 tips . . . . .1000 and up
Parabolic # 17 streamer fly rod - 2 tips . . . . .750 and up
Perfectionist trout fly rod - 2 tips . . . . .1500 and up

No. 32. Bait-Casting Rod. Made in two pieces. A new design in Bait-Casting Rods. Perfect in action for either accuracy or distance. Powerful enough to cast heavy plugs without tiring the wrist, but with plenty of whip for light lures. Has three genuine agate guides and genuine agate tip top. Lengths 4½, 5 and 5½ feet. Weight, about 6 ounces _____**Each $10.00**

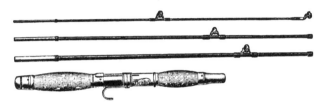

No. 33. Bristol Bait-Casting Rod is a light, elegant model; agates are selected with the greatest of care, the handle trimmings finished in a new finish trim, more durable than bright nickel, and much richer in appearance; the whole rod in every respect is made with the utmost care. Fitted with three narrow agate casting guides and a special design agate offset top. Double grip cork handle 14 inches long, with detachable finger hook. 4½, 5, and 5½ feet long. Weight about 8 ounces _____**Each $12.00**

No. 27. Bait-Casting Rod is built on the lines of the No. 33, but heavier weight _____**Each $11.00**

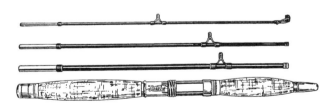

No. 31. "Bristol" Rod similar to No. 27, but with larger handle and joints made of heavier guage steel throughout. Length 5½ feet, weight 16 ounces, with double cork grip handle, one inch reel seat, large agate casting guides and offset agate casting top; 19½ inch handle, 18 inch joints_____**Each $14.00**

HEDDON "TEMPERED" SPLIT-BAMBOO FLY RODS

Heddon fly rods are made of flawless, thick walled, split (not sawed) bamboo and "tempered" by Heddon's special process which adds strength and rugged durability. Heddon rods are not undercut to fit each ferrule. This insures additional strength, smooth action and a perfect fit. These factors are why Heddon's are called the "Rods With The Fighting Hearts." Famous Heddon fly rods are the "Blue Waters," "Thoroubred," "Black Beauty," "Bill Stanley's Favorite," "Peerless," "President" and the "Rod of Rods," for presentations. Actions — extra light trout, light trout, standard trout, bass trout, power plus and heavy duty.

HEDDON "PAL SPOOK"® SOLID GLASS RODS

Heddon "Pal Spook" solid glass rods are designed for fishing, not to amaze people with trick demonstrations. They have flex where flex is needed to give long effortless, accurate casting, and backbone where power is needed to set a hook, and play a large fish.

Three grades available in 4, 4½, 5 and 5½ foot lengths and in Extra Light, Light, Medium and Heavy actions to suit all types of fishing. Only Heddon's exclusive process makes possible this selection of actions.

The foregrip has new style collet tip locking device that always fits tight, yet releases with a mere quarter turn.

All metal parts are durable and rust-proof, and grip is fine specie cork. Recognize the Heddon "Pal Spook" by the exclusive Red Butt Cap.

HEDDON "PAL"® REEL

Its light, sturdy construction assures smoother, longer casts. Users of Heddon "Pal" reels have won many state and national tournament events for accuracy and distance. Because of its exclusive removable head ring, it can be taken apart with a twist of the wrist, without using tools or changing a single adjustment — and reassembled just as easily. This greatly simplifies cleaning and oiling and assures free, effortless operation of this fine precision reel.

FISHING REELS

Casting and Big Game Reels

Uncomplicated crank reels of the Eighteenth Century were called "winches". The early winch was made of iron or brass and fitted with a screw clamp and wing-nut for rod retention. It has recently been determined that the first geared (multiplying) reel was of English origin, having been produced by hand about 1780.

Across the ocean George Snyder, a watchmaker and silversmith from Paris, Kentucky, created the first American multiplying reel in 1812. Snyder's designs were soon improved upon by craftsmen such as Jonathan and Benjamin Meek of Frankfort, Kentucky. The Meeks produced hand made reels apart from their established watch-making operation in the late 1830's to 1852. Benjamin Meek then worked with B.C. Milam for several years and in 1883 moved to Louisville to form a partnership with his sons. All types of Meek reels are highly desirable collectibles today - from the rare, early J.F. Meek to more common models such as the #33 *Bluegrass* - grab 'em while they 're still around!

The period from 1880 to 1900 certainly marks the golden age of American fishing reels. In addition to the "Kentucky" makers, quality casting reels were produced by Edward Vom Hofe, Julius Vom Hofe, Conroy of New York, and the Talbot Reel and Mfg. Co. of Kansas City, Missouri.

From the early 1900's through the 1930's, large companies such as Wm. Shakespeare Jr., Heddon. A.F. Meisselbach, Horton (formerly

Meek), The Enterprise Mfg. Co. (Pflueger), and South Bend Tackle Co. made great strides into the field of mass production and the use of level-wind mechanisms.

The Andrew B. Hendryx Co. of New Haven, Connecticut, a metal manufacturer (lures, bird cages, cat boxes, etc.) also distributed fishing reels and created many interesting, inexpensive designs.

After World War Two, some of the most superior , modern free spool reels were marketed. Among them were the famous Pflueger Supreme and Shakespeare President. Perhaps the best ever was the early Ambassadeur from AB URFABRIKEN (Abu) of Sweden. The 1950's - 1960's *Ambassadeur* and the lesser known Abu *Record* are still very desirable both as collectibles and usable casting or trolling reels.

Several decades after the Kentucky reel makers began producing freshwater bait casting multipliers, the pioneer New York makers such as J.C. Conroy, T. H. Bate, Thomas Conroy, Frederich Vom Hofe, and Julius Vom Hofe followed with heavy saltwater reels for east coat striped bass and bay fishing. Typical New York reels circa 1860 are solid brass with a "ball" style counter-balance handle opposite a rosewood winding knob. Civil War period antique reels are highly regarded examples of early American workmanship and are fast becoming museum pieces. Nautical collectors search these out as well.

In 1902, Edward Vom Hofe patented a "star drag" which was later utilized on the fine Vom Hofe 621 Series big game reels. Pflueger installed the "Williams" patent drag mechanism on large saltwater reels like the rugged *Alpine* model. These sturdy drags were a great boon to the tuna, marlin, and shark angler who previously relied on a leather thumber to slow down a fishes run.

In the 1920's and 30's, Julius Vom Hofe *B-Ocean* reels or J.A. Coxe 6/0 - 16/0 size reels were standard, high-end charter boat tackle, while Pflueger's many saltwater models provided an economical, yet good quality alternative. The finest saltwater big game reels ever made came from the small shop of Arthur and Oscar Kovalovsky, in North Hollywood, California. Little known to collectors only a few years ago, a custom Kovalovsky reel of the 1940's or 1950's is a treasure. It is safe to say that auction prices will continue to soar on these.

Fly Reels

The first reels used for fly fishing were small British crank designs called "pirns". Farlow, Alexander Martin, Malloch, and Hardy Brothers were English and Scottish makers that sold brass, wood, or silver fly reels during the nineteenth century. Beginning in 1891, Hardy produced the famous *Perfect* fly reel which to this day runs on a smooth set of ball bearings. The Perfect, although it is considered too heavy for modern tastes, set a high standard for quality single action fly reels. Hardy also manufactured the lighter *St. George* - very popular with collectors and contemporary fly fishers due to it's large capacity and perforated, lightweight spool. The St. George always came equipped with a patented agate line guide. Other excellent Hardy reels from the 1930 - 1950 period are the *Uniqua*, *Sunbeam*, and *St. John*. This era also yielded good English fly reels from Allcock (*Conquest*), Ogden Smith, Alex Martin (*Thistle*), Farlow (*B.W.P and Saphire*), and J.W. Youngs (*Beaudex, Pridex, etc.*).

Post Colonial American fly fishing began with the use of home-made or British equipment. In 1864, Thaddeus Norris, the best known American angling writer of the time, recommended a small two inch diameter click reel or "pirn" for most eastern trout fishing. It was not until the 1880's that American made fly reels found a place in the market. Orvis produced a simple, ventilated spool reel at this time, while Hiram Leonard sold a solid "raised pillar" design to go with his fine rods. Thomas Conroy and Julius Vom Hofe crafted exquisite, small trout fly reels of hard rubber side plates and German silver rims.

From 1895-1917, ventilated "skeleton" spool fly reels were distributed in large numbers by Meisselbach (*Featherlight series*) and Pflueger (*Progress*). The Progress came in a nickel or gun-metal (blued) finish and can be identified by a "bulldog" trade mark on the reel foot.

Arguably the most outstanding fly reels ever made were those of Edward Vom Hofe - *The Peerless, Perfection, Tobique,* and *Restigouche*. Vow Hofes were elegant hard rubber reels, silver rimmed with ornate serpent like handles. All are very collectible today and difficult to find in mint condition. Original Vom Hofe hard leather cases add much value when they accompany a reel.

The most common fly reel found by collectors is the Pflueger *Medalist*. It is the older "made in U.S.A" Medalists that are better quality and a bit more valuable. Many collectors praise this reel for it's durability and appealing drag, however I have found the drag to be jerky at higher settings and typically choose another of my reels for more delicate fishing. Nevertheless, a used Medalist is a good buy when you consider the price of a new American made reel today. Another reasonably priced reel to look for is the cheaper (no drag) circa 1950 Pflueger *Gem*. Actually the Gem is less available than the Medalist, so it shows more promise as a collectible. The Shakespeare *Russel* is a similar find.

Old Automatic spring-loaded fly reels are as abundant as real estate agents these days! It is pretty clear that, for now, all but the earliest automatics are practically without collectible value. The circa 1885 Yawman and Erbe reel (later H&I), Pflueger *Superex*, and the Meisselbachs are the best of the more valuable lot. Some collectors seem attracted to the first Martins with their 1923 patent, but they never exchange hands for much and can be easily found at most antique stores and flea markets. So if you like autos to collect or fish, horde a few because their value can only go up!

Spinning Reels

The Malloch sidecaster from Scotland, first produced around 1884, is considered to be the Grandfather of fixed-spool (spinning) reels. Then in 1905 came the odd shaped Illingworth *Mark One*. Later Illingworth reels and the Hardy *Hardex - Altex* reels, more closely resemble the spinning reels that we are familiar with today. Look for the older, half-bail style spinning reels for an unusual slant to your collection.

For the most part, the better, collectible spinning reels have European origins and are as follows: Mitchell (C.A.P. Co. of France), Allcock (England), Quick (West Germany), Luxor (France), and Alcedo (Italy). In addition to Alcedo's great Micron reels, they also made the excellent Orvis spinning reels of the 1960's.

The smoothest drag to be found on any spinning reel is affixed to the Zebco *Cardinal*. The circa 1970 Swedish-made Zebcos are prized by knowledgeable anglers and a real "sleeper" for collectors.

With the exception of Fin Nor's ultra-expensive, gold saltwater reel, the only notable American made spinning reels are the contemporary Penn *Spinfisher*, Pflueger *Pelican* (c.1955), and Bache Brown *Mastereel* (c.1949).

If you are starting a reel collection on a small budget, think about spinning reels from Europe or the U.S.

Buying Collectible Reels

Keep in mind that only reels in top condition will hold collectible value for a long time. A true antique reel (90 years old plus) or a rare reel may retain some value despite a rough appearance or broken parts, but is usually difficult to sell or trade. If you are determined to amass a collection of reels in "lower" condition and plan to keep each one forever - then this warning justifies little consideration! However, I know that most collectors love to trade or sell and "upgrade" their collections at some point. As the collector gains more experience, he or she may become dissatisfied with reels that seemed OK when purchased years before. Enough said about why condition is important.

When examining a reel to inspect it's condition, first look for any broken, missing, replaced or repaired parts. Screws, end bearings, and winding knobs are most common. Next look for cracks in the side-plates, holes drilled in the reel foot, a filed reel foot, or bent frame. Last, operate the reel to inspect the mechanical integrity. Of course, one of the defects mentioned may be acceptable to you and can be used as bargaining leverage!

A big "plus" in collectible value is discovering a reel in it's original box or leather case. If the original papers are enclosed, so much the better.

Old reels are everywhere! Garage sales, Antique shops, and Auctions. When you least expect it, a vintage Kentucky baitcaster or Hardy fly reel will turn up. I once bought (at a bargain price) a mint condition Edward Vom Hofe #621 reel in it's original leather case, at a flashy shopping mall "antique" show. I recently read a story about a tackle collector who regularly probes trunks of old cars at junk yards - with some success!

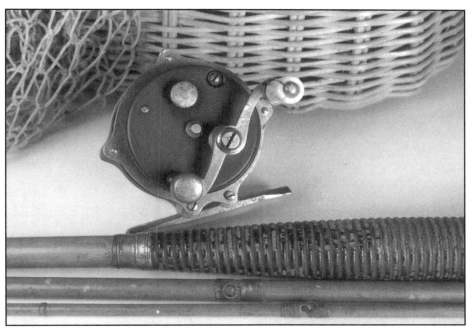

Trout reel c.1900 possibly made by Julius Vom Hofe. Greenheart fly rod with "flip ring" guides c.1880.

Barney & Berry - Winchester click reel and Montague hard rubber reel both c. 1915.

Small brass "pirn" raised pillar reel from Thos. Chubb.

B.C. Milam & Son Rustic #3 multiplying reel. Frankfort, Kentucky.

B.F. Meek and Sons #33 Bluegrass multiplyer made in Louisville, Kentucky.

ABU "Ambassadeur" limited edition gold reel, in original wood box.

South Bend level-wind bait casting reel of the 1950s.

Pflueger "Autopla" bay reel with leather thumb drag.

Civil War period brass, ball-handle reel made by J. Conroy of New York.

Edward Vom Hofe #621 big game reel - 6/0 size.

Carlton skeleton style fly reel, Rochester, New York c.1910.

Thompson aluminum fly reel with ball bearing drive.

Hardy Perfect fly reel - steel lineguide c.1950.

Hardy 3¹/₈" Uniqua fly reel with brass foot c.1935.

Mitchell 304 spinning reel imported by Garcia in 1962.

VALUE GUIDE
OLD FISHING REELS

Price ranges are for reels in excellent condition - all original parts, no repairs, showing signs of only moderate use and mechanically perfect. Reels in lower, well worn condition warrant a deduction in estimated value of as much as 50%.

Abu - Sweden
Ambassadeur #2600 (c.1958) . . . .$30 - 50
Ambassadeur #5000 (c.1965) . . . . .30 - 60
Record casting reel . . . . .35 - 60
Limited edition gold Ambassadeur (wood box) . . . . .400 - 550

Allcock - England
Conquest fly reel . . . . .40 - 85
Brass fly reel c.1890 . . . . .70 - 120
Stanley spinning reel c.1925 . . . . .90 - 150

Alcedo
Micron spinning reel . . . . .35 - 75
Larger spinning reels . . . . .25 - 45

Airex
Bache Brown spinning reels . . . . .15 - 30
Spinster model . . . . .10 - 20
Beachcomber spinning reel . . . . .12 - 25

Bristol
#65 fly reel . . . . .10 - 15
#66 fly reel . . . . .10 - 15

Bronson
Spinning reels - most models . . . .$6 - 10
Casting reels (average) . . . . .6 - 12

Carlton
Automatic fly reel c.1915 . . . . .50 - 90
Lightweight model fly reel . . . . .35 - 65

Thomas Chubb
Brass pirn (c.1890) . . . . .25 - 50

Conroy
Brass antique bay reel c.1850 - 1860 . . . . .400 - 800

Cozzone
Silver and hard rubber casting reels . . . . .90 - 150

J.A. Coxe
10-2 casting reel . . . . .18 - 30
15-C casting reel . . . . .15 - 25
25 casting reel . . . . .30 - 50
25-N casting reel (narrow spool) . . . . .45 - 65
6/0 - 9/0 size big game reels . . . . .150 - 350
625 saltwater bay reel . . . . .15 - 35

Farlow - England
BWP fly reel c.1930 . . . . .70 - 125
Saphire fly reel c.1960 . . . . .40 - 65
Early brass Salmon reel . . . . .95 - 175
Brass pirn crank reel   c.1880 .75 - 130

Fin Nor
Fly reels (saltwater) "wedding cake" style . . . . .300 - 500
Gold Spinning reel . . . . .150 - 250

Hardy - England
Elarex casting reel . . . .$75 - 115
Jock Scott casting reel . . . . .275 - 390
Brass Perfect fly reel c.1900 . . . . .400 and up
1928 - 1960 Perfect with brass foot . . . . .175 - 275
St. George fly reel . . . . .150 - 250
St. John fly reel . . . . .100 - 160
Uniqua and Sunbeam fly reels .65 - 150
Hardex and Altex spinning reels .40 - 100
Silex reels . . . . .125 - 300
Fortuna big game fly and trolling reels . . . . .400 and up

Horrocks - Ibbotson
Average casting reel . . . . .8 - 12
Utica automatic fly reel . . . . .4 - 8
Yawman and Erbe early automatic . . . . .40 - 80
average spinning reel . . . . .5 - 10

Heddon
Spin - Pal c.1950 . . . . .15 - 25
Imperial #125 fly reel . . . . .35 - 65
Chief Dowagiac casting reel . . . . .60 - 95
Lone Eagle casting reel (level-wind) . . . . .40 - 60
Model 3-15 casting reel . . . . .125 - 175
Model 3-25 casting reel c.1927 .95 - 150

Andrew B. Hendryx
Small brass reel with no gears . . . . .12 - 20
Casting reels . . . . .30 - 40
Raised Pillar brass fly reels . . . . .15 - 30

Illingworth - England
First model #1 spinning reel c.1905 (in case) . . . . .300 - 500
Later model spinning reels . . . . .50 - 135

Kovalovsky
Big game reels . . . .$1000 and up

Langley
Spinlite and Spinflow spinning reels . . . . .6 - 15
Speedcast and Plugcast casting reels . . . . .6 - 15
Model #340 Target casting reel . . . . .20 - 40

Leonard - Wm. Mills Co.
H.L Leonard 1877 patent click fly reel . . . . .400 - 700
Mill's Fairy trout fly reel (2") . . . . .450 - 800
Leonard model #50 fly reel . . . . .400 - 700
Leonard fly reel c.1984 . . . . .250 - 400
Wm. Mills and Son c.1940 salmon reel . . . . .125 - 175

Luxor - France
#1 spinning reel c.1950 . . . . .30 - 55
Larger models . . . . .20 - 45

Liberty Bell Co.
Liberty Bell reel (c.1905) . . . . .350 and up

Martin
Automatic fly reel (1923 patent) .8 - 20
Automatic fly reel #27 c.1940 . . . . .5 - 12
Flywate fly reel c.1960 . . . . .5 - 12

Meek (and Milam)
J.F. Meek c.1835 -1840 casting reel . . . . .2500 and up
J.F. and B.F. Meek c.1840 - 1851 . . . . .1700 and up
Meek and Milam c.1851 - 1878 .600 and up
B.F Meek and Sons #2 (tournament size) . . . . .265 - 450
B.F. Meek and Sons #3 . . . . .175 - 275
Horton - Meek (later) #3 . . . . .150 - 215
Carters Patent #33 Bluegrass . . . . .75 - 120

B.C. Milam (Frankfort Ky.) . . . .$375 and up
B.C. Milam and Son (i.e. "Rustic") . . . . .150 - 250
Horton "Meek" #56 fly reel . . . . .60 - 90

Meisselbach
Tripart and Takapart casting reels c.1910 . . . . .18 - 35
Okey #625 casting reel . . . . .40 - 75
Symploreel #255 casting reel . . . . .50 - 80
Flyer (level-wind) c.1928 . . . . .20 - 30
Featherlight fly reels (#250) 1904 patent . . . . .25 - 45
Featherlight fly reels (#280) 1896 patent . . . . .30 - 50
Expert fly reels (i.e.#13,#19) 1886 -89 pat. . . . . .35 - 70
Rainbow fly reel #627 . . . . .10 - 20
Cattucci fly reel #370 . . . . .35 - 70
#660 early automatic c.1920 . . . . .40 - 75
Neptune saltwater bay reel . . . . .35 - 70
"Good Luck" wood pier reel c.1900 . . . . .45 - 75

Mitchell - Garcia
Early C.A.P spinning reels . . . . .20 - 40
"Spinette" (c.1955) . . . . .6 - 12
#300 and #302 (made in France) . . . . .12 - 30
#308 ultra-light (made in France) . . . . .15 - 35

Malloch - Scotland
Sidecaster c.1890 (blued brass) . . . . .125 - 200
Salmon reels c.1920 . . . . .100 - 195

Montague
Clipper and Atlantic saltwater bay reels . . . . .10 - 20
Offshore and Longbeach ocean reels . . . . .20 - 35
Early hard rubber click reel (Vom Hofe "style") . . . . .20 - 40
Imperial 6/0 big game reel . . . . .95 - 150

Ocean City

Fortesque (nickel-silver) bay reel	$25 - 50
Bay City ocean reel c.1941	10 - 20
Ike Walton saltwater reel	40 - 70
Long Key 6/0 big game reel	40 - 70
Balboa 10/0 big game reel	145 - 190
Panama (10/0 - 14/0) c.1938	150 - 210
#300 and #350 spinning reels	10 - 20
#35,#36,#76,#77 fly reels	6 - 15
Wanita fly reel	4 - 8
X-pert fly reel	10 - 20
#90 Automatic fly reel	6 - 15

Orvis

1874 trout fly reel (some in walnut box)	350 - 800
CFO fly reels	40 - 90
Model 50 ultra-light spinning reel (Italy)	30 - 45
Model 100 and larger spinning reels	20 - 35

Pflueger

Gem fly reel (early model)	20 - 35
Gem #2094	8 - 20
Medalist fly reel (made in U.S.A.)	20 - 40
Sal-Trout fly reel (early brass)	20 - 35
Sal Trout #1554	8 - 20
Progress fly reel (early bull dog mark)	15 - 30
Progress #1744	6 - 15
Golden West fly reel c.1930	100 - 185
Supreme #578 fly reel	60 - 95
Superex #775 automatic fly reel c.1910	40 - 60
Four Bros. Delight fly reel	65 - 125
Akron #1893 casting reel	10 - 20
Buckeye (07,23 pat.) early	40 - 65
Skilcast #1953	12 - 25
Summit #1993 casting reel	15 - 35

Supreme #1573 casting reel . . . .$25 - 40
Trump #1943 casting reel . . . . .8 - 15
Worth (early c.1915) . . . . .35 - 55
Four Bros. Capitol (60 yard size) . . . . .12 - 20
Four Bros. Regal casting reel . . . . .10 - 20
Atlas - Portage and Portage Topic #123 . . . . .15 - 30
Alpine saltwater reel (With Williams drag) . . . . .40 - 80
Atlapac 6/0 big game reel . . . . .85 - 125
Avalon big game reel (1907 patent) . . . . .60 - 110
Adams big game reels . . . . .125 and up
Oceanic bay reel (1907,23 pat.) . . . . .30 - 50
Everlaster bay reel . . . . .30 - 50
Pontiac saltwater reel (1921 pat. wood brake) . . . . .30 - 50
.Temco (1923,26,27 pat.) . . . . .15 - 30
Sea- Vue bay reel c.1940 . . . . .10 - 18
Norka bay reel . . . . .15 - 30
Ohio and Bond bay reels . . . . .18 - 35
Rocket #1375 ocean reel . . . . .15 - 30
Taxie trolling reel (Ferris wheel design) . . . . .10 - 20
Sal - Trout #1558 trolling reel . . . . .10 - 20
Pelican spinning reel . . . . .15 - 30

Penn
Early c.1939 with wood handle knob . . . . .15 - 25
Later models (Squidder,#209, #155) . . . . .20 - 35

Quick - Germany
Early D.A.M. model spinning reels . . . . .20 - 40
Later models c.1970 . . . . .15 - 35

Shakespeare
Russel fly reels . . . . .15 - 25
Sturdy fly reel model #1861 . . . . .10 - 20
Ausable fly reel . . . . .18 - 35
Automatic fly reel #1847, #1821 .8 - 18

Kazoo (early skeleton spool) fly reel .... $20 - 35
Acme #1904 casting reel .... .8 - 15
Criterion #1961 casting reel .... 15 - 25
Ideal #1963 .... 10 - 20
Marhoff casting reel .... 15 - 30
Professional #1965 casting reel .... 18 - 35
Service reel (c.1905 Wm. Shakespeare Jr.) .... 40 - 75
Tournament (free spool - narrow spool) .... 40 - 75
Sportcast #1973 (c.1955) .... 10 - 20
Sportcast #1977 (narrow spool) .... 30 - 45
True Blue #1956 casting reel .... 10 - 20
Uncle Sam casting reel .... 15 - 30
Universal #2 (Wm. Shakespeare Jr.) .... 35 - 70
Wondereel .... .8 - 18.
President #1970 A (c.1955) .... 15 - 30
Miller - Autocrat big game reel .... 135 - 200
Jupiter (nickel silver bay reel) .... 30 - 60
#1960 surfcasting reel .... 15 - 20
Service (star drag ocean reel) .... 18 - 30

South Bend
#350,450,550 and 750 casting reels .... .8 - 15
#1000 (early) .... 15 - 20
#1200 (c.1920 high quality level-wind) .... 20 - 40
Finalist fly reel .... .8 - 12
St. Joe fly reel (skeleton design) c.1920 .... 25 - 35
Oreno automatic fly reel .... .5 - 8
#850 surfcasting reel c.1940 .... 10 - 20

Talbot
Kansas City, Mo. casting reels .... 175 - 350

Edward Vom Hofe
Freshwater multiplying reels (1896 patent) .... 200 - 300
Perfection fly reel c.1900 .... 1500 and up

Peerless fly reel (1883 patent) . . . .$900 and up
#504 "Tobique" . . . . .500 and up
#423 "Restigouche" . . . . .400 and up
Model #560 saltwater reel . . . . .125 - 275
Model #521 saltwater reel . . . . .165 - 300
Model #621 big game reel 6/0 . . . . .150 - 295
Model #621 big game reel 9/0 . . . . .200 - 350
Model #721 "Commander Ross" . . . . .400 and up

Julius Vom Hofe
German-silver and hard rubber fly reels . . . . .175 - 275
All metal trout fly reel (1889 patent) . . . . .200 - 300
Casting reels size #1, 2, 3, hard rubber . . . . .65 - 125
Nickel plated - brass bay reel ('89 patent) . . . . .60 - 95
"B - Ocean" big game reels (1911 patent) . . . . .150 - 275

Frederich Vom Hofe
Pre-Civil War antique brass bay reel . . . . .900 and up
Civil War era (Clover leaf TM - Julius) . . . . .500 and up

Winchester
#4142 casting reel . . . . .65 - 90
Barney and Berry early fly reel .50 - 80
#2830 saltwater bay reel . . . . .50 - 80
Winchester early raised pillar fly reel . . . . .75 - 115

Wright & McGill
Fre-line #16 spin reel . . . . .6 - 10

Wordens
Belt Reel c.1953 Granger WA. .45 - 65

J.W. Youngs - England
Ambidex spinning reel . . . . .35 - 50
Beaudex fly reel . . . . .30 - 55

Condex fly reel . . . .$20 - 35
Pridex fly reel . . . . .35 - 70

Zebco
Cardinal spinning reels (Sweden) . . . . .25 - 50
Zero Hour Bomb spin reel . . . . .15 - 25
Model #22 spin reel c.1950 . . . . .5 - 15

FISHING LURES

Bass Plugs

Although chronologically metal spoons and rigged spinners came first, it is the wood plug, and primarily the bass plug, that constitutes the root of many lure collections today.

On September 20, 1859 the *Riley Haskell Minnow* was patented. Only a handful of these valuable lures exist today and the known examples have a silver-plated copper body. Nevertheless, the Haskell Minnow is worthy of mention as a "plug" because the original patent application lists wood as a possible body material. If a legitimate wood Haskell is found it will be worth mega-bucks!

H.C. Brush Co. of New York, produced a "Floating Spinner" patented in 1876 with a wood or cork spinner rig. Then in 1883, inventor Harry Comstock patented the *Flying Hellgrammite* lure with a real wood body and metal "wings". Authentic Flying Hellgrammites are one of the top collectible lures in the world.

The original wood bass plug, as we know it, must be credited to James Heddon. Around 1890 Mr. Heddon discovered the potential of floating wood lures when one of his discarded whittling projects was attacked by a largemouth bass. Shortly thereafter, Heddon began hand carving crude frog shaped lures for himself and friends. The actual Heddon factory started ten years later.

From the time of the Heddon Company and it's famous *Dowagiac Minnows* (1904), other large manufacturers entered in to the plug business. The Pflueger *Simplex*, *Monarch*, and *Globe* have proven to be extremely popular early plugs. William Shakespeare Jr. of

Kalamazoo, Michigan offered the *Revolution* bait and *Rhodes Wooden Minnow* - all in full production by 1910.

From about 1915, South Bend Bait Company of Indiana was developing a strong lure selection with the *Underwater, Surface,* and *Panatela* Minnows. The famous *Bass-Oreno* came along about this time and started the extensive "Oreno" line of lures that endured for years.

Creek Chub Bait Company of Garret, Indiana began the marketing of it's great plugs with the *Wiggler* in 1911. Later came the famous *Pikie* (1930's), *Plunker,* and *Beetle.* One of CCBC's most widely used bass plugs is the *Injured Minnow* (referred to in a 1930 Field and Stream ad as the "Crippled Minnow"). As with all Creek Chub baits, they come in a variety of colors and sizes; the most common is a natural perch scale with red gills.

Dozens of plug companies formed over the years from 1920 - 1950, including Bite-em Bait Sales, Woods of Arkansas, Eger of Florida, Jamison, and Paw Paw.

Even though some of the early plugs mentioned above are worth hundreds of dollars, a great attraction to the hobby of lure collecting is the fact that a nice group of wood plugs can still be put together for a reasonable amount of cash! Examples are the following 1950's plugs; all can be had in the $10 - $20 range (a bit more in the original box). Make sure they are made of wood, and not later plastic versions. Some might have glass eyes, but painted eyes are OK:

Heddon - Crazy Crawler, Basser, Lucky 13.
Arbogast - Wood Jitterbug.
Creek Chub - Injured Minnow, Pikie.
Woods - Doodler.
Shakespeare - Dopey, Swimming Mouse.
South Bend - Bass Oreno.
Pflueger - Mustang.
Paw Paw - Wounded Minnow

Metal Lures

The first metal lures pre-date the use of wooden plugs by fifty years. A multitude of spoons, spinners, minnows, and devons from North America and Great Britain have been produced since the early 1800's, in brass, silver, and copper.

One of the first metal lures was the original homemade "spoon" of Julio T. Buel (actually a silver dinner spoon with a hook on it). In 1849, Buel started a manufacturing company in New York. Pflueger, Eppinger, Wilson, McMahon, and others followed with complete product lines.

A few years after the advent of spoons, came the spinner. The spinner offered a versatile alternative for many game fish. Spinners were fished alone or rigged with a feathered hook or buck-tail fly. They could be cast or trolled.

A very collectible pre-1900 spinner is the Skinner brand with it's engraved 1874 patent date. J.E. Pepper of New York, The "Chicago" Spinner (1903), and Chapmans of Rochester are others. The Hendryx Company of Connecticut was also a big player in metal lures from the 1890's to about 1910.

Salmon trollers in the Pacific Northwest, utilized the *Pop Geer* spinner blades in tandem followed by a herring or lure. Rigging the blades in a "gang" simulated a school of bait fish and served as an attractor.

During the 1930's and 40's, metal lures were extensively marketed for trout, bass, and pan fish. Some of the more popular lures in the original cardboard boxes or screw capped tubes are great collectibles. Examples are: Johnson *Silver Minnow*, the first *Dardevles* (Eppinger), Arbogast *Tin Liz* (baitfish shaped), and the incredibly effective South Bend *Trix-Oreno*. Certain metal lures, such as the Trix-Oreno, were available in the miniature, fly rod size. Metal fly rod baits are a collection in themselves and an interesting specialty to pursue!

Metal devons were designed to look like a sleek baitfish and resemble a spinning torpedo in the water. The first were made in England. Firms such as Hardy, Pflueger, and Horrocks-Ibbotson sold them in various sizes and colors. I have even seen tiny fly rod devons.

One of the weirdest of the metal clan is the Al Foss line of "wig-glers" and spinners. About 1916, Foss began selling the *Little Egypt Spinner* for pork rind rigging, followed in 1920 by the *Oriental Wiggler* (a pork rind - plastic minnow). Early Al Foss lures came enclosed in an attractive tin box with lovely old graphics. I find these boxes to be more appealing than the strange looking lures!

Metal lures of the 1950's and 60's have not yet become very valu-able. 1950's Mepps spinners, for example, might be a future col-lectible - so put a few away and fish the rest.

Salmon Plugs

Prior to the introduction of wood salmon plugs, trollers used regu-lar bass lures or spoons to catch silver and king salmon from the oceans, bays, and sounds off the Pacific Northwest coast. Lures like the Heddon *Basser* were great fish getters, but the weak hooks straightened out or broke off on big kings. A few anglers started to modify the bass lures with heavier hooks, or began carving their own stout plugs by hand. As demand increased, local northwest entre-preneurs began producing true salmon plugs. One of the first was the Jack Lloyd (circa 1928), followed by Martin of Seattle, Hanson, Roseguard, Nelson, and L.E. Olsen of Bellingham.

Large manufacturers got into the act during the 1930's and 40's, marketing plugs suited for salmon and larger game fish. Primarily advertised for catching salmon, striped bass, and muskellunge, these sturdy plugs were cast and trolled for tuna, yellowtail, and bonito as far south as Mexico and the Sea of Cortez. Heddon *King Zig Wags* and *King Bassers*, in addition to the *Giant Vamp* series, are particular-ly collectible due to lower production numbers than smaller regular bass plugs.

Buying Old Fishing Lures

Quite often, lures are discovered in a tackle box and a collector will pay a reasonable lump sum for the whole lot, averaging the cost of each lure. This is a good way for the new collector to get started. Be aware that the value guide at the end of this chapter is a rough indicator and does not include variations for scarce colors or age. If you are just new to collecting, stay within the lower price ranges, unless you can afford to overpay.

When examining a lure, especially a wood plug, look for loose hardware, re-painted body, replaced or broken hooks, missing or chipped eyes, tooth marks, and excessive age cracks. These all effect value and the amount you might want to pay. Even a partial re-paint can render a lure worthless as a collectible.

Finding a lure in it's original cardboard box is a plus. Many come with enclosed small catalogs. Some of the earliest lures were packages in jointed wood boxes. These are very rare, and collectible on their own. If you are paying extra for a box, try to make sure it is the correct one for that lure. In the old days, plugs would get mixed up on the tackle shop shelf or placed in the wrong box after fishing.

Early metal lures - The Chicago Spinner and The Skinner rigged spinner bait.

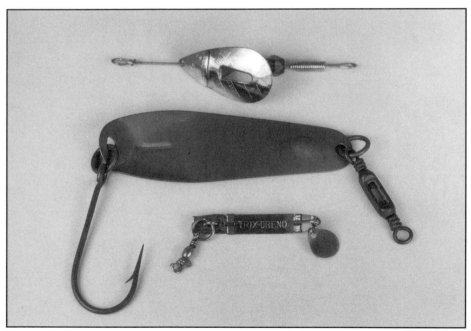

Pflueger June Bug Spinner (top), McMahon Spoon, and South Bend Trix-oreno.

Pflueger Star spinner made of brass prior to 1930.

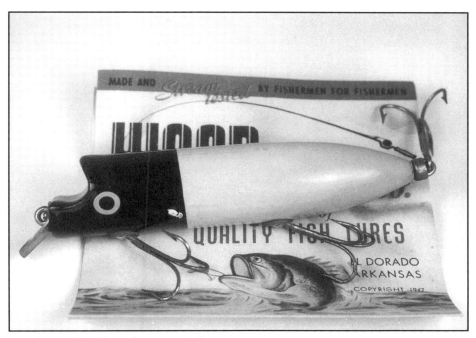

Woods "Doddler" bass plug circa 1949.

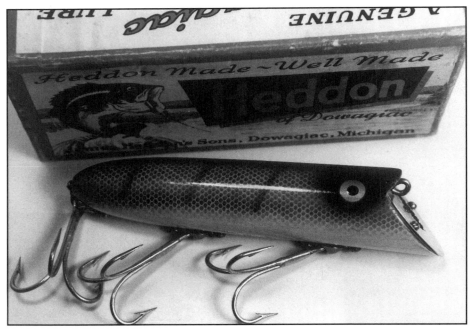

Heddon "Basser," later model with painted eyes.

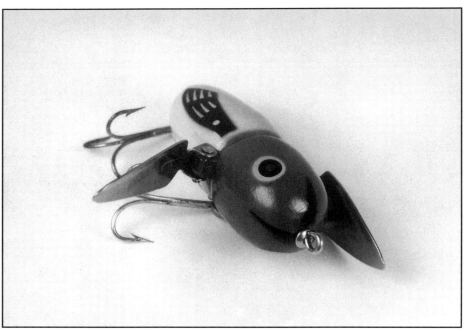

Heddon "Crazy Crawler" surface plug c.1955.

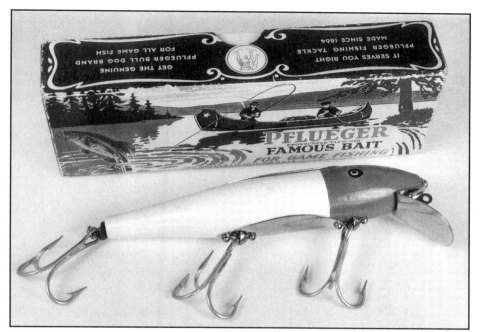

Pflueger "Mustang" - large diving plug of the 1940s.

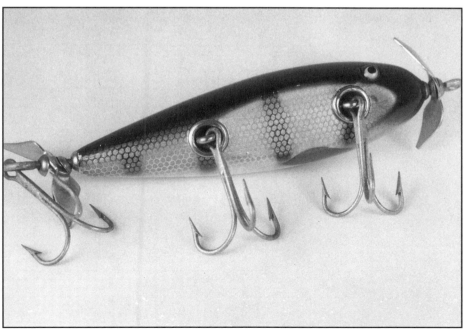

Creek Chub "Injured Minnow" bait with glass eyes.

Martin jointed salmon plug made in Seattle, WA.

Small-size Martin salmon plug circa 1950s.

VALUE GUIDE
OLD FISHING LURES

Listings are for lures in excellent condition. Worn condition may be 30-50% lower. Mint in the original box may be 25-40% higher.

Allcock - England
Metal devon . . . .$15 - 30

Arbogast Co.
Jitterbug (wood) . . . . .6 - 15
Tin Liz (metal) . . . . .45 - 75
Hula Popper (plastic) . . . . .2 - 4

Bite - Em Bait Co.
Bate . . . . .75 - 95
Lipped Wiggler . . . . .90 - 130

J.T. Buel
First design 1852 patent spoon (Whitehall,NY) . . . . .75 - 125
Later J.T. Buel Co. spoons and spinners . . . . .10 - 30

Chapman & Son
Allure #1 or #2 . . . . .135 - 175
Pickerel Spinner . . . . .60 - 85

Comstock
Flying Hellgrammite (rare) . . . . .1200 and up

Creek Chub Bait Co.
Ding bat . . . . .12 - 22
Beetle . . . . .30 - 65
Injured Minnow . . . . .12 - 20
Pikie . . . . .10 - 20

Plunker . . . .$12 - 20

Decker
Topwater . . . . .60 - 95

Eger Bait Mfg. Co.
Torpedo . . . . .20 - 40
Dillinger . . . . .8 - 15
Bull Nose (frog skin) . . . . .20 - 40

Eppinger
Early Dardevle (in cardboard box) . . . . .3 - 6

Flood
Florida Shiner . . . . .200 and up

Al Foss
Little Egypt Wiggler . . . . .5 - 10
Oriental Wiggler (in earliest green tin box) . . . . .40 - 65
above in the later red tin box . . . . .15 - 30

Hastings
Wilson's Wobbler . . . . .25 -65
Wilson's Six-in-One Wobbler . . . . .150 - 200
Wilson's Winged Wobbler . . . . .45 - 75

Haskell
Original 1859 Minnow (very rare) . . . . .3000 and up

Hardy - England
Devon (average) . . . . .20 - 45

James Heddon
Artistic Minnow . . . . .100 and up
#100 Minnow . . . . .25 - 95

#150 Minnow . . . .$50 - 100
#210 Surface Minnow .20 - 45
Slope Nose Expert (surface bait) . . . . .100 and up
Lucky 13 . . . . .12 - 25
Basser . . . . .10 - 20
King Basser (salmon plug) . . . . .20 - 40
Crab Wiggler . . . . .30 - 55
Baby Crab . . . . .20 - 40
Crazy Crawler . . . . .12 - 20
Wilderdilge (fly rod) . . . . .15 - 30
Gamefisher . . . . .20 - 40
River Runt Spook (plastic) . . . . .5 - 8
Punkinseed . . . . .25 - 45
Dummy Double (rare) .300 and up
Loony Frog . . . . .35 - 55

Hendryx
Spinner rigged with feathered fly . . . . .12 - 20

Jamison
Shannon Twin Spinner . . . . .3 - 6

Johnson
Silver Minnow . . . . .3 - 6

Keeling
Expert Minnow (c.1905 - 1920) rare . . . . .200 and up
Tom Thumbs . . . . .40 - 75

Martin
Salmon Plugs (Seattle, WA.) average . . . . .6 - 20

McMahon
early patented spoons . . . . .2 - 6

Moonlight Bait Co.
Pikaroon . . . .$75 - 95
Fish Spear (c.1916) rare . . . . .250 and up

National Bait Co.
Bass King (c.1929) . . . . .80 - 100

Olsen
Salmon Plugs (average) . . . . .10 - 30

Paw Paw Bait Co.
Wotta-Frog . . . . .25 - 55
Wobbler . . . . .10 - 15
Pike Minnow . . . . .15 - 20

Pepper
Early spinners (c. 1900) . . . . .25 - 45
Wood plugs (most) . . . . .150 and up

Pflueger
Pal-O-Mine . . . . .12 - 20
Globe . . . . .15 - 30
Mustang . . . . .15 - 25
Neverfail Minnow . . . . .45 - 85
Kent Frog . . . . .175 and up
Surprise . . . . .150 and up
Simplex . . . . .100 - 150

Rush (U.S. Specialty Co.)
Tango Minnow . . . . .25 - 60

Shakespeare
Wood Revolution (c.1901) rare . . . . .700 and up
Revolution (pre-1920 aluminum) . . . . .150 and up
Rhodes Mechanical Frog . . . . .200 and up

Swimming Mouse . . . .$10 - 25
Slim Jim . . . . .20 - 40
Pop-Eye . . . . .12 - 20
Frog Skin bait (real skin) . . . . .60 - 85
Midget Spinner . . . . .10 - 20
Dopey . . . . .6 - 12
Wooden Minnow (c.1912) . . . . .65 - 95

Skinner
1874 patent spinner with feather or bucktail . . . . .25 - 45

South Bend Bait Co.
Coast-Oreno salmon plug . . . . .25 - 45
Mouse-Oreno . . . . .15 - 25
Bass-Oreno . . . . .7 - 20
Tease-Oreno . . . . .18 - 40
Pike-Oreno . . . . .10 - 20
Surf-Oreno . . . . .10 - 25
Panatela Minnow . . . . .15 - 30
Woodpecker (early) . . . . .25 - 40
Ketch-Oreno (fly rod size) . . . . .8 - 15
Vacuum Bait (formerly Howe's) .50 - 110

Union Springs
Miller's Reversible Minnow (rare) . . . . .1000 and up

Winchester
Multi-Wobbler . . . . .175 and up
Minnow (3 or 5 hook style) . . . . .250 and up
Spinner rigged with feather fly . . . . .20 - 40

Woods
Doodler . . . . .12 - 20
Spot Tail Minnow . . . . .10 - 15

FLY FISHING COLLECTIBLES

Trout, Salmon, and Bass flies

Artificial flies are as abundant, it seems, as their natural counterparts. Numerous old leather wallets, with musty smelling felt pages, grace the bottom of tackle boxes everywhere. Old, second-hand trout flies have very little or no value, unless they can be authenticated and identified as having been tied by a "known" angler. If the original purchaser of the flies can attest to their providence, an appraisal by an experienced collector or museum curator may still be necessary to assign any value to a loose fly or set. A "known" angler is normally not the next door neighbor who used to catch lots of fish. Most collectors will only pursue flies tied by recognized authors or commercial fly-tiers. This is not to say that beautiful, framed sets of flies by a local artist are not valuable - but this is "art" value not "fly" value.

Highest prices are paid for the work of legendary anglers. Preston Jennings, Carrie Stevens, Syd Glasso, Ruben Cross, Harry Darbee, and Roderick Haig-Brown all command great attention. Glasso anadramous patterns and authentic Jennings or Stevens streamers trade hands at two hundred dollars and more.

Contemporary fly fishing authors occasionally make their flies available to collectors through book signings, special programs, or personal contacts. If a note or letter from the author is attached, an everlasting authentication has been made. A limited edition book, signed by an author, may include a fly affixed to the title page, above the signature. In any case, this is an economical, risk free way to start a collection of flies from known, present day authors.

Sylvester Nemes' soft hackle flies; Randall Kaufman, Gary Borger, or Polly Rosborough nymphs; Dave Whitlock bass flies; Ralph Wahl, Bill McMillan, Dick Van Demark, or perhaps Trey Combs steelhead flies; Darrel Martin CDC's; Swisher-Richard no hackles; Rick Hafele mayflies; and Gary LaFontaine caddisflies are just a few examples of modern, collectible flies that might turn up.

Antique gut-eyed Atlantic Salmon flies from Europe make beautiful framed displays. Long-ago unavailable, exotic materials adorn these works of art wound upon blackened hooks. No providence is necessary for gut-eyed flies to be collectible (Value $15 and up), yet those enclosed in the original waxed paper envelope or embedded in the makers card, peak a collector's interest. Look for retailers such as Hardy and Farlow. Modern individual maker's like Scotland's Megan Boyd, Spain's Belarmino Martinez, and contemporary American craftsman Steve Gobin's patterns are framed and not fished! (this is understandable since their intricate, large flies sell in the $50 - $100 range).

William Mills, L.L. Bean, and Orvis all sold packaged single and assorted flies. Most have a collectible value of $3 - $6 if still enclosed in the original wrapper with company logo.

Inexpensive "spinner-flies" were sold for many years by Hardy (*The Halcyon*), Allcocks, and Pflueger. A wired blade or prop was placed forward of the fly (often weighted), producing a good combination lure that could be cast with a fly rod, spinning rod, or trolled. Part of the attraction to spinner-flies are the bright graphics that usually appear on the header card. Needless to say, flies like this, on the original card, hold more value ($3 - $6, Hardy's $10 - $15).

Fly Boxes and Leather Wallets

Partitioned aluminum fly storage boxes are highly collectible, and practical as well for modern use. Sturdy boxes were made under the Allcock, Hardy, Ogden Smith, Farlow, and Wheatley brand names - all of British origin. Wheatleys continue to be produced today and remain the best grade available. Interior designs varied, ranging from simple clips to clear, hinged lids. Some fancier boxes included tweezers for removing small flies, slates for writing the fly pattern names, and even bound-in entomological charts. Several English boxes from the 1930's displayed an exterior of imitation tortoise shell. These *Neroda* style boxes can be worth in excess of $50 in good condition with no chips. Aluminum boxes made prior to 1940 can be worth anything from a few dollars to seventy-five, depending on features and size. The most valuable are early (pre-1910) blackened aluminum boxes (which are getting more difficult to find in clean condition with no dents).

Leather wallets with pages of wool, imitation felt, or paper were made in North America and abroad. Numerous designs and sizes were available. Look for real leather and quality workmanship. Although there are many interesting, inexpensive wallets to be found (i.e. *Common Sense Fly Book*, Montgomery Wards, etc.), only a true antique, handmade wallet from around the Victorian period is worth the forty dollars or more asked by dealers. The leather covers, and especially the parchment pages of these, were often abused by contact with water and consequent mildew. It is a rare pleasure to find a vintage fly wallet in perfect condition. So if you come across one with no water marks, rotten pages or broken clasps - don't pass it up!

Hardy gut-eyed atlantic salmon flies and leader.

Steelhead fly tied by angling author Ralph Wahl.

English aluminum fly box with tweezers. Pflueger "Progress" reel c.1920.

Leather fly book made in Oregon around 1939.

THE H. & D. FOLSOM ARMS CO., 314 BROADWAY, N. Y. — Distributers

PFLUEGER PILOT FLY *SPINNER*
Trade Marks Reg. U. S. Pat. Office—Patent Nos. 272317-468361-564839

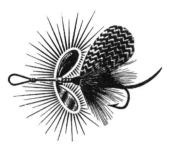

Sneck Hooks—Bright Tin Plated, hand filed out points, Size 8. Pilot Fly Spinners are mounted with our famous Tandem Spinner blade and do wonderful work with trout and bass wherever they may be found. Cast with either a fly or bait casting rod.

Flies are tied true to standard patterns and we carry the flies as listed below. A wonderful killer—a *breath* will spin it.

Black Gnat	Montreal
Brown Hackle, Peacock Body	Professor
Coachman	Red Ibis
Gray Hackle, Peacock Body	Royal Coachman
Grizzly King	Reuben Wood
Yellow Sally	White Miller

Spinner Size 3/0

Assortment consists of 12 Spinners, one each above patterns.

No.	Price Per Assortment
1828 Polished Nickel Both Sides of Blade...	**3.00**

Packed—Displayed on fine printed cards. One assortment (one dozen spinners) in a card box.

FISHING ACCESSORIES AND TERMINAL TACKLE

Hooks

Authentic, early hooks that were handmade by ancient indigenous peoples, from rock, bone, or ivory, are museum relics and now almost impossible to find for sale. The 15th century manuscript *Treatyse of Fysshynge wyth an Angle*, attributed to Dame Juliana Berners, described the process of hook making and the application of silk and soft hackles to produce a basic wet fly. American pioneers and settlers are known to have fashioned their hooks from bent pins or needles. In the 19th and early part of the 20th century, hook manufacturers such as Allcock of England and O. Mustad and Son of Norway helped develop both the hand forged and bent wire methods of hook making.

Some tackle collectors seem to be drawn more to the interesting containers that hooks were sold in, rather than the hook itself. Odd shaped tins with colorful logos and small paper boxes with graphic labels, make hook collecting all the more fascinating. Old Pflueger brand hooks were packed in wood, cylinder shaped boxes with the famous bulldog label on top.

Certain hooks were snelled on gut leaders and packaged on cardboard sheets, while others came enclosed in glassine or waxed paper sleeves.

A circa 1930 - 1960's box or tin of hooks can usually be purchased for about three to five bucks, with older hooks ranging to $10 per box (larger salmon hooks or unusual fly tying hooks may go at a premium).

Leader and Line

Old silk worm gut leaders and lines are gaining popularity as collectibles. English and American conventional gut leaders in waxed paper sleeves are attractive and inexpensive. English gut fly fishing leaders, with fancy envelopes may be worth as much as five dollars. The Hardy brand fly leaders are worth a bit more, and come complete with a registration number and company seal.

Usable silk fly lines are sought by collectors of early split bamboo rods, because the guides on some of these antique rods are too small to accommodate modern, tapered synthetic lines. The cost of a new silk fly line is astronomical, so anglers look for old lines to clean and use.

Many spooled lines for bait casting and saltwater (*Cuttyhunk Brand*) were of the cotton or linen variety and are pretty common. However, high quality, spooled silk lines for tournament casting are getting much harder to locate and can be worth $8 or more in fine condition. Make sure the original paper labels are attached, and that all the proper yardage is intact. Ashaway, South Bend, and Wilson are but a few of the tackle companies that sold spooled lines either individually or inter-connected.

Bobbers

Colorful floats or "bobbers" made of quill, cork, or wood were an important piece of equipment for fishermen wishing to keep their bait off the bottom and free of snags. They also served as an indicator of the strike. In addition to the simple float, through which the line passed, manufacturers during the first part of the 20th century created some unusual variations (bobbers that whistled, lit up, and rang!).

The largest manufacturer of bobbers, in the United States, was the Ideal Float Company of Richmond, Virginia. Ideal's output was known as the *Cadillac of Bobbers*. Most consisted of a brightly paint-ed cork cylinder with a birch-wood stick through the middle, topped with a rounded wood line adjuster (usually painted red).

Ideal floats were offered in either barrel or egg shape. Older examples (c.1918) exhibited a carved knob on top of the stick to prevent the brass line guide from coming off.

Colors of Ideal floats from 1920's were red and green, white and green, fancy stripes, and plain cork finish.

A large bobber of this type (body of approximately six inches) is prized by collectors and can bring $25. Collectors pay $3 - $10 for average size bobbers (body of two to four inches).

Akin to a bobber, at least in shape, is the casting plug or practice plug. Most were made of rubber but a few, such as the South Bend brand were painted wood (just like a bass plug) with a lead insert. Practice plugs like this came with some of the better tournament casting reels of the time (1915 - 1930). In the case of the South Bend brand, the practice plug is now worth as much or more than the model #1200 reel with which it came.

Split-Shot Containers

Pinching "Split-Shot" (lead shot) has always been a convenient way to add weight to fishing line without re-rigging. In recent years, fortunately, some manufacturers have developed non-lead shot to protect lakes and streams from environmental damage. Surprisingly, the old shot containers, made of metal, are becoming inexpensive, popular collectibles. Look for Pflueger, H&I, Meadow Brook, and Ideal brands in clean condition - these are worth about three bucks and are fun to display in a collection of terminal tackle.

Creels and Fish baskets

Whole or split willow creels from Europe and the eastern United States were favored angling accessories during the late 19th and early 20th centuries. Unfortunately, most creels and trout baskets were not labeled, making it tough to distinguish between an authen-tic 80 or 90 year old Adirondack craft work and a cheaper copy from the orient. A twenty year old, mass produced creel may look older than it's actual age due to natural weathering. Look closely for "made in China" markings or processed leather trim. An honest, antique creel is hard to find, so collectors and decorators gladly pay $40 - $80 and more for an example with the leather closure or wood peg in good repair. Contemporary creels are worth considerably less.

Native American fish baskets are discovered on occasion. These ancient museum pieces, made of woven twig or vines, command great attention at antique auctions and often reach several hundred dollars before the bidding ends.

Desirable "named", western made creels are the Lawrence and Macmonies brands - fetching prices in excess of $100 in good condition.

English suppliers like Hardy, incorporated a sectioned bag into their creel design. An example is the *Trout Fisher's Bag* from the 1938 Hardy catalog and Angler's Guide. Similar bags have sold at auction in recent years for as much as $150. Around 1899 Hardy proudly advertised an extra large creel that came with a fly wallet snapped to the inside of the lid, and a special compartment for the angler's lunch!

Landing Nets

Many old trout and salmon landing nets are discovered at garage sales, antique shops and auctions. The most common is the *Harrimac* design from L.M. Richardson Co. of Chicago (also a maker of roller skates). Richardsons usually have a wood handle (painted black or natural wood grain) that screws onto a steel net frame as it is expanded. Value of an average net like this is $10 or $15 for trout size, $30 and up for salmon size with a longer, sectioned wood handle. Of course, if the original netting is in poor condition you should pay less.

Hardy Bros. of England produced their famous *Royde* landing net in the years before World War One. The Royde was in the shape of a triangle and came fitted with a fish weighing attachment, combined with a wading staff or folded with a portable fishing seat!

Expect to pay good money (about $150 - $200) for a net of this Caliber in excellent to mint condition.

"All wood" trout nets of solid or laminated wood strips are collectible and functional as well. With the cost of new, American made hardwood nets now over $50, a good used net from the 1950's or 60's is a very practical buy at half the price.

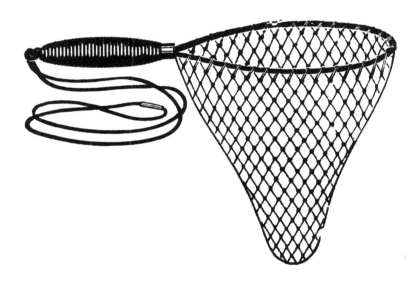

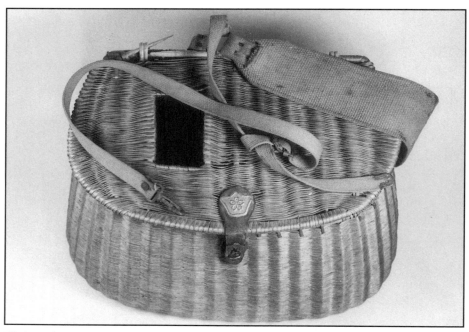

High quality American made creel with harness.

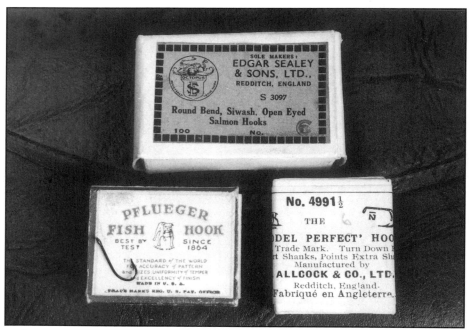

Collectible bait and fly tying hooks.

1950s Cortland fly line and small fly rod baits.

Collectible split-shot containers 1930-1950.

Beautiful old cork bobber and Folsom 1931 tackle catalog.

ANGLING EPHEMERA PAPER COLLECTIBLES

Fishing Tackle Catalogs

Old catalogs are very useful for researching the background of rods, reels, and tackle. Older catalogs are filled with rich artwork and nostalgic line drawings. Paper collectibles (ephemera) are difficult to obtain in superior condition since many were destroyed, burned for fuel, or used as toilet paper. The best catalogs contained various articles on new tackle and techniques. Hardy's Angler's Guides represented the classic example of promotion and advertising for the tackle industry of that time. (1890's - 1950 and later) It must have been hard to resist making a purchase from those beautiful little books.

Large American retailers and outfitters such as Folsom Arms, VL&A, Orvis, Norm Thompson, and L.L. Bean also did a big portion of their business through mail-order. Most of these catalogs are excellent listings of the best gear available in the particular year of the issue.

Major tackle manufacturers made new catalogs available to consumers each year, by mail. Small brochures or leaflets were often included inside the box with a reel or lure. Pflueger and Heddon printed many small "pocket" size catalogs during the 1950's and 60's.

Fishing Tackle Catalog Value Guide

$100 or more...

Hardy Angler's Guide (prior to 1928)
Early C. Farlow & Son Ltd
Edward Vom Hofe (1898 - 1950)
Julius Vom Hofe (circa 1900)
Abbey and Imbrie (1900 and earlier)
Charles F. Orvis (circa 1900)
Early Thomas and Leonard rods
Meek reels
Winchester (early)

$50 - $100...

Hardy Angler's Guide (1928 - 1940)
Abercromby & Fitch (early)
Abbey & Imbrie (circa 1920)
Creek Chub Bait Co. (circa 1930)
Folsom Arms (circa 1930)
Horton - Bristol rods and reels (1910 - 1930)

$25 - $50...

Shakespeare (1930 - 1940)
Heddon (circa 1930)
Pflueger (1920 - 1940)
South Bend Bait Co. (prior to 1940)

$15 - $25...

South Bend (1940 - 1950)
Hardy (circa 1960)
Heddon Pocket Catalogs
Orvis (1950 - 1960)
L.L. Bean (1950 - 1960)
Weber
Montague
Horrocks - Ibbotson

American Outdoor Magazines

Fortunately, old outdoor magazines (despite the fragile nature of paper) are still available to collectors as a result of large print runs and the common practice of keeping back issues. Many fishermen and hunters, carefully stored past issues of their favorite magazines in a garage or attic for future reference.

The most ancient of North American outdoor periodicals, American Turf Register and Sporting Magazine, was published during the 1830's and 1840's. It included numerous articles on horse racing, as it's title suggests, but also covered the subjects of fishing and hunting. Good copies of these early magazines are scarce and quite valuable.

In the later part of the 19th century, magazines like The American Angler and Forest and Stream were popular. These issues are getting more difficult to locate in better condition, as the age of the paper reaches over one hundred years. Look for clean smelling copies (no mildew) with light or white page stock. Old periodical and book pages can develop "foxing" or dark spots. If the magazines were stored at room temperature, in a dry place, chances are they will be in superior condition.

Issues of Field and Stream, Outdoor Life, and Hunting and Fishing from the 1920's to 1950's and regional magazines like The Alaska Sportsman can be collected at a moderate price. Many of the cover designs were painted by well known wildlife artists of the time, such as Lynn Bogue Hunt, Hy Watson and Fred Everett.

Old magazines not only offer information about classic fishing destinations and techniques, but also provide an excellent resource for details about old fishing tackle. The old reel and lure advertisements "speak" to a collector, as if to say - "you have to find one of these" or "I've never seen that model before".

Certain issues of fly fishing magazines from the 1960's and 1970's have now become collectible. Complete "early" runs of Fly Fisherman and Fly Fishing the West (now Flyfishing) are being seen on dealer lists.

Look for old magazines at antiquarian book fairs, used book stores, and antique shops. Prices range from a few dollars on up. The best source, however, for magazines in good condition is a reputable book dealer who specializes in periodicals, such as Lou Razek of Highwood Bookshop in Traverse City, Michigan.

Fishing Books

Many fishermen read about their sport in magazines and outdoor newspapers, however a growing number of anglers purchase books, both hardcover and paperback, pertaining to individual fishing methods and equipment. Fly fishermen have available, hundreds of titles in print from which to choose. In addition to these current publications, the inquisitive angler can discover a wide range of classic, out of print books. Due to the limited or small print runs of some of the older books (and even some recent hard cover first editions), collectors are having a hard time finding the best titles at used book stores - a source that was brimming over with great buys as little as ten years ago! Therefore, if you should come across a personal library of quality fishing books or stroll into a used book store that has just purchased one, it might be wise to buy a box-full while you can.

The traditional source for top grade angling books has always been the specialty dealer. Expect to pay top dollar for books in fine or better condition - but it may be well worth it, considering the scarcity of some titles.

An excellent reference for anyone interested in fishing books is Angling Books of the Americas by Henry Bruns. Mr. Bruns, who privately published this gem in 1975, lists virtually any book, that even mentions sport fishing, from a North American publisher up to 1970. Sadly, Hank Bruns recently passed away and I am not aware of any plans to reprint this great resource. A used book dealer can possibly locate a copy through a "book search".

Fishing Book Value Guide

A varied sampling of authors and titles are listed below, with broad value guidelines based on average dealer prices. All are hard-cover bindings, most are first editions in clean, fine condition with dust jackets if applicable.

Arbona, F. Mayflies, the Angler and the Trout (1980) . . . . .$20 - 25
Bates, J. Atlantic Salmon Flies and Fishing (1970) . . . .$50 - 80
Bergman,R. Freshwater Bass (1946) . . . .$25 - 35
          Trout reprint (1950 - 1970) . . . .$13 - 18
Brooks, C. Nymph Fishing For Larger Trout (1976) . . . .$20 - 25
          The Trout and the Stream (1974) . . . .$25 - 30
Brown, J.J. American Angler's Guide (1845) . . . .$150 - 300
Combs, T. Steelhead Fly Fishing and Flies (1976) . . . .$30 - 40
          The Steelhead Trout (1971) . . . .$45 - 55
Dunne, J.W. Sunshine and the Dry Fly (1924) . . . .$50 - 60
Flick, A. Streamside Guide (1947) . . . .$40 - 50
          Streamside Guide reprint (1960's) . . . .$6 - 10
Grant, G. Montana Trout Flies (1981) Lim. ed. . . . .$55 - 65
Grey, Z. Tales of Fresh Water Fishing (1928) . . . .$80 - 125
Hafele, R. Complete Book of W. Hatches (1981) . . . .$45 - 60
Haig-Brown, R. The Western Angler (1939) 2 Vol. . . . . . .$600 +
          The Western Angler (trade ed.) . . . .$55 - 75
          Fisherman's Fall (1964) . . . .$50 - 60
Halford, F. Floating Flies & How to Dress Them (1886) . . . . .$150 +
Henshall, J. Book of the Black Bass (1902 reprint) . . . .$50 - 55
Hewitt, E.R. Secrets of the Salmon (1922) . . . .$40 - 45
Jennings, P. A Book of Trout Flies (1935) Lim. ed. . . . .$650 +
          A Book of Trout Flies (1960's reprint) . . . .$30 - 35
Kaufman, R. Lake Fishing with a Fly (1984) . . . .$40 - 50
Keane, M. Classic Rods and Rodmakers (1976) . . . .$70 - 90

La Branch, G. The Dry Fly & Fast Water (1914) . . . .$65 - 70
Lampman, B.H. A Leaf From French Eddy (1965) . . . .$25 - 30
              Coming of the Pond Fishes (1946) . . . . . .$35 - 40
Leisenring, J. Art of Tying the Wet Fly (1941) . . . .$60 - 70
              Later edition with V. Hidy (1971) . . . .$15 - 25
Marinaro, V. A Modern Dry Fly Code (1950) . . . .$50 - 75
              A Modern Dry Fly Code (1970 reprint) . . . .$15 - 20
Nemes, S. The Soft Hackle Fly (1975 first ed) . . . .$50 - 60
Norris, T. The American Angler's Book (1875, 2nd) . . . . .$95 - 110
Orrelle, J. Fly Reels of the Past (1987) . . . .$35 - 45
Raymond, S. The Year of the Angler (1973) . . . .$20 - 25
              Kamloops (1971) . . . .$40 - 50
Rhead, L. American Trout Stream Insects (1916) . . . .$75 - 85
Rosborough, P. Tying & Fishing the Fuzzy Nymph . . . .$15 - 20
Schaldach, W. Current and Eddies (1944) . . . .$35 - 50
Schweibert, E. Matching the Hatch (1955) . . . .$45 - 55
              Matching the Hatch (1971 reprint) . . . .$18 - 25
              Nymphs (1973) . . . .$40 - 45
Scott, G. Fishing in American Waters (1870's 2nd) . . . . . .$85 - 95
Skues, G. Way of a Trout with a Fly (1928 2nd) . . . .$60 - 75
Trotter, P. Cutthroat (1987) . . . .$20 - 25
Vernon, S. Antique Fishing Reels (1985) . . . .$20 - 25
Wahl, R. Come Wade the River (1971) Limited ed. . . . .$200 - 300
              Come Wade the River (trade edition) . . . .$75 - 95
              One Man's Steelhead Shangri-la (Lim. ed) . . . .$50 - 60
Walton, I. Complete Angler reprints 1890 - present . . . . . .$15 - 90

Hardback, out-of-print fishing books from 1914 to 1970.

Fishing and outdoor magazines prior to 1940 are tough to find in mint condition.

WINCHESTER

SPLIT BAMBOO FLY RODS

HOP BROOK

Rod of handsome brown treated stock. Has nickel silver fittings. File hard steel snake guides. Solid ringed cork grip. Nickel silver angle tip. Attractively wound at guides and fittings. Machine welted serrated waterproofed ferrules. Extra tip joint. Tips in protecting tip holder. Packed in partitioned canvas bag.

Number	App. Weight	Length
6030	4 ¾ oz.	8 ½ ft.
6035	5 ¼ oz.	9 ft.
6040	5 ¾ oz.	9 ½ ft.

KILDE

Rod of handsome brown treated stock. Has nickel silver fittings. Screw reel seat. Solid ringed cork grip. Butt guide of imitation agate. Others file hard steel snake guides. Machine welted serrated waterproofed ferrules. Steel angle tip. Attractively wound at guides and fittings. Extra tip joint. Tips in bamboo tip case. Packed in partitioned canvas bag.

Number	App. Weight	Length
6043	4 oz.	7 ½ ft.
6044	4 ¼ oz.	8 ft.
6045	4 ¾ oz.	8 ½ ft.
6050	5 ¼ oz.	9 ft.
6055	5 ¾ oz.	9 ½ ft.
6060	6 ¼ oz.	10 ft.

POMPERAUG

Handsome brown treated stock rod. Has nickel silver fittings. Screw reel seat. Solid ringed cork grip well fitted to the hand. Machine welted serrated waterproofed ferrules. First guide is of one ring type of genuine agate. The others are of file hard steel. Angle tips, one Roto-ring, the other of file proof, hardened steel, nickel plated. Attractively wound at guides and fittings. Bamboo used in this rod is scientifically treated to produce fine action, and strips are matched so that knots will not come together. Extra tip joint. Packed in partitioned canvas bag. Aluminum rod case.

Number	App. Weight	Length
6065	4 ½ oz.	8 ½ ft.
6070	5 oz.	9 ft.
6075	5 ½ oz.	9 ½ ft.

A page from an early Winchester catalog.

ABOUT THE AUTHOR

Dan Homel sold and repaired fishing tackle as a part-time job while attending college. He has been collecting, trading, and studying old tackle since his senior year in high school (1972). After being employed as an attorney and corporate sales executive during the 1980's, Dan now works in the literary field. A member of the NFLCC, he has two other books currently in print: *Diary of Northwest Trout Flies*, and *Collector's Guide to Old Fishing Reels*.

Ask your local Bookseller for:

Collector's Guide to Old Fishing Reels - 96 pages. Historical data, collecting tips, and value guidelines for 425 different reels dating from 1840 - 1970. Fifty detailed B&W photographs. Covers casting, spinning, American and British fly reels, big game and unusual reels! Fascinating information for beginner and experienced collector alike. (Forrest - Park Publishers ISBN: 1-879522-01-2)

Diary of Northwest Trout Flies - 96 pages. Detailed patterns are presented for 35 productive Pacific Northwest trout flies. These are local favorites, old reliables, and a few of the author and illustrator's own designs. Each fly was drawn, in pen and ink, by wildlife artist Ed Ruckey. Tying and fishing notes are included! (Forrest - Park Publishers ISBN: 1-879522-00-4)

APPENDIX

The National Fishing Lure Collectors Club

The National Fishing Lure Collector's Club (NFLCC) is the largest organization of fishing tackle collectors in the world. Members collect all types of tackle, not just lures as the name would seem to indicate. Membership extends beyond the United States to Canada, England, France, Sweden, Japan, Holland, and the Netherlands.

The United States is split into "regions" and each area holds a yearly "meet" where members get together to display, trade and sell old tackle. A quarterly newsletter is published, along with a color magazine. If you are at all serious about collecting tackle, joining the NFLCC has it's benefits!

For membership information contact:

Secretary NFLCC
Kit Wittekind
P.O. Box 13
Grove City, Ohio 43123

Publisher's Note

(A) The analysis and opinion of value expressed herein is meant only as a basic guideline for hobby collectors, and is the subjective view of the author. Independent investigation of value is recommended before any transaction or speculation for profit. The publishers have included what we feel to be a good sampling of collectible fishing tackle, however there are literally thousands of other rods, reels, lures, tackle and variations thereof, to be found. Enjoy the search!

(B) Correspondence to the author may be made through the publisher by writing:

Dan Homel
C/O: Forrest - Park Publishers
5187 Ranchos Road
Bellingham, WA 98226

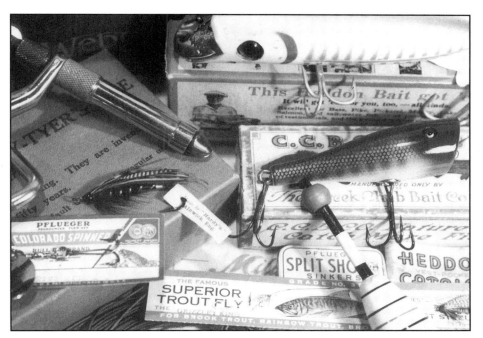

(Clockwise from top) Heddon "King Basser," CCBC "Plunker," Ideal bobber, a gut-snelled fly, Colorado Spinner, Hardy fly and original Thompson fly tying vise.

Scarce "Liberty Bell" reel with unique free spool mechanism activited by the winding knob.